HOW TO TRACE YOUR IRISH ROOTS

le
Nora Ní Aonghusa

Published by:
Michael and John Hennessy
Tankardstown, Kilmallock, Co. Limerick,
Ireland.

To the memory of
my loving parents,
John and Mary Danaher (nee Hennessy)
also
my husband's parents
James and Johanna Hennessy (nee Maunsell)
and
all my ancestors, who inspired me to
put pen to paper.

First published 1986
Reprint 1987

Printed by Litho Press Co., Midleton, Co. Cork.

CONTENTS

LIST OF ILLUSTRATIONS

HOW IT ALL BEGAN FOR ME

All my life I have had a burning desire to construct a "Family tree" but it was one of those things I just never semed to get round to doing. Anyway there was plenty of time to do it later on, there were still plenty of relations alive to give me all the information at some later stage. While I was growing up I always seemed preoccupied with something more urgent, dates etc., and enjoying all the good things of my teenage years. Next came marriage and children, God bless them, so my family tree was forgotten about again.

Then about five or six years ago, when my favourite aunt died, it suddenly occurred to me that most of my family, that is, parents, aunts, uncles, and far out cousins, had gone to their final resting place and if I did not do something about trying to trace my family roots pretty quickly there would be no-one left to give me any information. Therefore I finally made up my mind to have a go at getting some information together.

At this stage also my children were asking me questions about their great grandparents and other relatives and I felt ashamed of not being able to answer their questions. This really did it.

I had no idea where to start, because like most people when I was young I always found my talkative grandparents and grandaunts and uncles very boring. If only I had realised all those old people who so loved to talk were precious mines of information. One should always LISTEN; it costs nothing and one can learn more from those custodians of tradition than one will ever learn from books, etc. It also makes them happy to find some young boy or girl interested in them and what they have to say, especially about when they were young.

I would be reluctant to put in writing how I started to try to trace my ancestors, but I can tell you this, I wasted very much time and money on telephone calls, writing paper and stamps, petrol in driving from place to place, and I found out very very little . Finally I sought some professional help and I can assure you that made a difference. he did not do any of the work for me, it would have cost too much - but he gave me some very useful advice, for a pretty reasonable fee, and it certainly made things much easier. At least, now I knew where to begin, just as I had spent so much with such little results that I had nearly given up the idea altogether. It is only now I realise how sorry I would have been, had I given up.

Now I am going to try to help you, using my own experience and mistakes as a guide line. I am going to tell you in my own words, so I hope you will be able to follow me, and if I jump from one thing to another, please forgive me; but I do hope you will also enjoy the pleasure of doing the research yourself. It really can be a lot of fun. It may work out pretty expensive at times; it will all depend on how much information you have already. At this point I must warn you that most families will have had a Black Sheep somewhere in their past, so do not be too surprised if at some stage along the line, you find out that all your lovable ancestors were not quite the Saints that you had hoped for. Personally I think if one comes up with something unexpected it makes one's search far more interesting and enjoyable. So Good Luck and enjoy your research! You are probably starting something you will be adding bits of information to for the rest of your life and something your children will thank you for.

Now before you make your trip to Ireland, that is, if you hope to come to follow up your work, it will be far better to try and do a little bit of research at home. It will also give you so much more time to enjoy yourself when you finally reach Ireland.

Now to start. If you have parents, grand-parents, aunts, uncles, even the proverbial 31st. cousin, or anybody else who may be able to give you any information, ask them to tell you everything they know, that may be of value to you in your research. It may well surprise you all the information you will get by just asking a few ques-

Emigrants leaving Queenstown at the turn of the century . (Courtesy of the National Libary)

tions and you will find it much easier to try to piece things together in the comfort of your own home.

I expect you already know that Ireland is an island consisting of thirty two counties, each county is sub-divided into cities, towns, and townlands. A townland is the smallest area of land in Ireland, it can range from two to one thousand acres but in general the average town-land consists of about four hundred acres. Now there are other divisions as well, ecclesiastical divisions, as the name suggests these divisions are Church divisions. These, like the counties, are sub-divided into smaller divisions, the larger is called the Diocese and the smaller is called a Parish. A parish is made up of a number of townlands and in cities there can be several Parishes.

To find our where your ancestors lived, you first need to know the county next the townland and finally the Parish. The fact that a great-grandparent Thomas Murphy came from Ireland is of no value and trying to trace his family would be like looking for a needle in a haystack, as it is most likely a couple of hundred Thomas Murphys would have left Ireland on an emigrant ship about the same time as your great-grandfather. So you need more information than this to find out where he originally came from.

You at least need to know from which county he came from, and even with this information it may still be difficult to trace his family, as in some counties there can be so many families of the same name, especially names like Murphy, McCarthy, O'Brien, O'Connor and Hennessy. These are some of the more common names in Ireland. Sometimes one can connect a particular name with a particular county. Let us take a name like McCarthy, it would be most likely that they at some time lived in Cork. Another name, Danaher - this we would associate with west County Limerick. There are several good books which give very useful information about Irish names and the most common names in each County.

As I said earlier one of the best sources of information is some elderly relative still living. Failing this, the best source to consult is the death certificate of the person whos roots you are trying to trace. In many death certificates you can find a considerable amount of information. In many cases the county in Ireland from where he or she came is stated, and even though this is not a lot, it is a start. You should also look at marriage certificates, because in most of these the names of the parents are given, at least in most cases the father's name and this would be of great importance when looking up records in Ireland. In some cases, a "Family Bible" may have been kept and this often would be a treasure as the townland of the original settler may be referred to.

In death and marriage certificates also you would be able to get the age of the person concerned, so you now would have the approximate date of birth. I say approximate because I have found, that in quite a lot of cases the correct age may not appear on the certificate, so when you are doing your search in Ireland do not confine yourself to a particular year. You can allow a few years on either side of the date given.

You can also refer to the immigration entry forms in your own country, but unfortunately I have found in many of these lists, there is very little information. You may get something like this - Thomas Murphy arrived port of Boston, July 1st. 1834 on ship St. James, country of departure Ireland. In some cases possibly in the case of the better off families, there may be much more information given. But sad to say, most of the normal run of emigrants would have left home with very little, they would even have gone for the want of work and food, especially during the mid eighteen hundreds on account of the Great-Famine. Thousands of starving Irish people left home during this period, seeking their fortune in the New World.

I will give some useful addresses of places you can contact in this respect later on.

IRISH RECORDS

In Ireland records may not be as informative as those in other countries. Many important documents and records were lost in a great fire in Dublin in 1922. Fortunately some were saved and can be inspected by the general public on request.

State records begin in Ireland in 1864, so if you are tracing somebody after this date, you could be lucky by just writing to the County or City Registrar of the particular county, that is of course, if you are lucky enough to know from which county your ancestor came. There is a search charge for this service. You would need to know the name of your ancestor and the Christian name at least of the father and if possible the maiden name of the mother. You may already have this information from a death or marriage certificate.

At this time I might add that most children would have been born at home. Which brings a problem, in that many such births were never registered. It may be that some people may have had suspicions about giving too much information to the authorities and of course it should also be remembered that many of the ordinary people were illiterate. Well whatever the reason, quite a numbr of births were never registered with the State. With marriages it would have been different, as these would have been registered by the Parish Priest of the Church in which the marriage took place. Again unfortunately, some Parish Priests appear to have had a little difficulty in accustoming themselves to the carrying out of the law, but this happened in only a few cases.

Let us assume that you are trying to discover the roots of your great grandfather. Let us call him Thomas Murphy and assume he arrived in the new country in 1830. Now we will again assume, you heard he had come from

Cork. On his death certificate you find he was 70 years of age when he died, so from this you know he was born (approximately of course) in 1810.

Let us again assume that you heard, from a relative, when you were making your earlier research that Thomas spoke of a place called "Mallow". As it happens Mallow is a lovely town in the county of Cork.

It would not be assuming too much, that you might hear the name of a town or place like this, as most of our ancestors would have spoken frequently about their beloved Parish or town in Ireland.

In the case of Mallow, here we are very lucky, because in this particular town the Church records go back to 1757. All you would have to do now is write to the Parish Priest at Mallow, County Cork, giving him the information you already have and ask for his assistance to follow it up. In doing this we are again assuming that Thomas was of Roman Catholic stock, so the record you would be getting here at Mallow, would be of his baptism, as he would likely have been baptised in the local Parish Church.

Likewise if he had been Protestant or other persuasion you would contact the Rector of the Parish in question.

Not all Church records go back as far as 1757. I will have a list later on of the Parishes in each county. Unfortunately most country records do not begin until late seventeen or early eighteen hundreds. This varies from one Parish to another. In this case, from the records at Mallow, that Thomas, son to Patrick Murphy and Brigid Murphy (nee Ryan) was baptised June 5th. 1811.

Sponsors:- John Murphy and Nora Ryan. Now at this point let us assume there is a very kind and helpful Parish Priest in Mallow, who is good enough to look back in the Church records, to find that Patrick Murphy, son of Thomas, and Brigid Ryan daughter of James, were married in this Church July 9th 1808. One can therefore go back another generation in this case as the records allow, that is if you wish to do so. But you may be more interested in tracing relatives that may be still living.

Now you might like to take note at this point, that it

was the custom at that time, to call the first son after the paternal grandfather, and the second son after the maternal grandfather. The eldest and second daughters were similarly named after the paternal and maternal grandmothers.

This custom is sadly not being observed and today many children are called after television personalities and film stars, rather than members of their families. I suppose it is all a matter of opinion but to my mind, there is no greater honour one can give loving grandparents than to name one's children after them.

I will show later, a chart somewhat like what you might get back from our friendly Parish Priest. It will be a great start to your "Family tree" and you will be happy to find you still have some long lost cousins still living in the old homestead.

Needless to mention no matter how kind our Parish Priest may be, he has to live also, and a small gift might be appropriate. Of course much will depend on how much work he has had to do. All the old Church records are written in Latin and the quality of the writing may not make if very easy to read. It can be a most exhausting and time consuming labour to follow up old records.

Now with our sample research so far we may have been very lucky, but I am sorry to say that in many cases it is not as straightforward as this. If for instance you are aware, that your great-grandfather, was born 1810 in County Cork, but you do not know in which Parish you could try a letter to the newspapers of the county in question. In this case the best would be "The Cork Examiner". You should send all the information you already have. The editor is nearly always happy to publish when he receives such a letter, as it will make interesting reading.

Such a letter will nearly always get results. I will not say the results will always be accurate, but in general Irish people find it hard to resist a letter bearing their surnames. Such a letter has often proven very furitful so you certainly should not overlook trying this.

I will give a list of all the larger Irish provincial newspapers later. These papers are mostly weekly and most Irish homes will get a copy of their own county's weekly newspaper.

EXAMPLE FAMILY TREE

Patrick Murphy married Brigid Ryan July 9th. 1808.

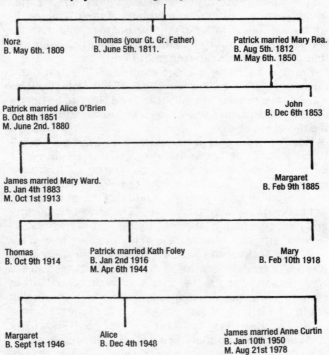

Nora
B. May 6th. 1809

Thomas (your Gt. Gr. Father)
B. June 5th. 1811.

Patrick married Mary Rea.
B. Aug 5th. 1812
M. May 6th. 1850

Patrick married Alice O'Brien
B. Oct 8th 1851
M. June 2nd. 1880

John
B. Dec 6th 1853

James married Mary Ward.
B. Jan 4th 1883
M. Oct 1st 1913

Margaret
B. Feb 9th 1885

Thomas
B. Oct 9th 1914

Patrick married Kath Foley
B. Jan 2nd 1916
M. Apr 6th 1944

Mary
B. Feb 10th 1918

Margaret
B. Sept 1st 1946

Alice
B. Dec 4th 1948

James married Anne Curtin
B. Jan 10th 1950
M. Aug 21st 1978

Here you have your cousin James and his wife Anne, with possibly their family still living in the same old homestead your Great Grand-Father Thomas left so many years ago.

B. - Baptised. M. - Married.

Cottage, Coast Road, near Doolin, Co. Clare.. (Courtesy of Bord Fáilte)

WHAT YOU CAN DO IN YOUR OWN COUNTRY

As I have stated earlier, the more homework you can do in your own country the better. I mentioned marriage and death Certificates and living elderly relatives. You might also check the gravestones of the original settler. Sometimes you may find a reference to the old country on such a stone. It may just be the county in Ireland where he originally came from. Every little bit of information helps to bring all the pieces together.

Assuming you have done all this, your next stop will be the Archives in your own country, as here you will find the immigration entry forms and most of the passenger lists. In America you will find these in the United States National Archives in Washington.

The Archives house two different types of list. The first is the customs passenger list. In this you will find, name, age, sex, occupation, country of departure and port of arrival. In the case of a passenger dying during the voyage details of the circumstances of death will also be given. It must be remembered that in those days, the ships were far from the luxury liners we have today and our ordinary Irish emigrant would have travelled third class and, as I said earlier, their health may have been far from good in the first place, so it is no wonder that many died on the journey. In fact, I have often heard these ships referred to as coffin ships. It appears that the conditions on them were so bad, that they were not suitable for animals, much less humans. It appears that the boarding houses, both in Ireland at Queenstown (now called Cobh) and also at the port of arrival, were so appalling that it does not bear thinking about. It was the conditions on such ships and boarding houses that led a County Limerick lady, Charlotte Grace O'Brien to try

18

to do something to improve matters. She set up a boarding house of her own at Queenstown, much to the dislike of the ship owners. She had already tried to get shipowners to improve conditions for passengers without any success, so then she decided by having her own boarding house, she could at least advise the emigrant as to the best ships to travel on.

All passengers were literally bundled into the same compartment men, women, and children, married and single all alike. Sleeping conditions were appalling. Miss O'Brien's main aim was to improve sleeping conditions for the single girls and also those of married couples. She also advised that a priest should accompany each emigrant ship with the hope that he would have some say in the treatment of the passengers.

Following a lot of hard work, she did achieve some results, both on the ships and the accommodation in the boarding houses, on both sides of the Atlantic. Many of our ancestors were much indebted to this fine lady. It would take a book to give a full account of her work. but to get back to our passenger lists.

The second list, the immigration passenger list gives somewhat the same information, but here one might get the placename of the birth place of the passenger. Also it might give the name of the last place he resided before leaving home. In some places also one might be lucky enough to get the name and address of a relative of the passenger in his home country.

The information one may get here is good but again you face another problem. You need the name of the ship your ancestor arrived on and also you require the port of embarkation and most important the date, or as near as possible. The Archives will do a search for you, if you have the above information, but a person can do his own research by examining the microfilms available there. If one has a lot of time it may be well worth trying this. You may well get excellent results.

More very useful information that can be referred to in the Archives as well, is the Census returns. These were taken every ten years from 1790. Until 1850, the head of the household only was noted. After this date there is more information, the name, age, and sex of each person in the house and most important of all, the place of birth. In this case as well, the Archives will be happy to assist in the search. This, in my mind, is really worth trying while at the Archives or while you are in touch with them, if your ancestor was given some land in the public land States, there should be a record of this also. Furthermore he would probably have become a citizen or applied for citizenship and you will get this information here also, so it certainly should not be overlooked.

While many of our ancestors went to the New World of America during the mid eighteen hundreds some others chose Australia. Some went as free agents, some were assisted by the State but many a poor man, woman and child were deported from their native land for some crime or other. It is hard to think today about the terrible suffering and torture our ancestors experienced. Some left their families, wives and children knowing they would never see them again in this life or never again step on their own native soil. I heard of one girl, who at the age of ten years, was deported for seven years, her crime was stealing a bedspread. The poor girl never again saw her family. When she was finally given her freedom she married another Irish convict. They made a good life for themselves together, they worked hard and bought some land and reared nine children. She was just one of the thousands who were sentenced to Van Dieman's land (now Tasmania) or New South Wales for petty crimes. Thank God those days are gone.

In Australia as in America are the National Archives to help you trace your roots. Most Australians probably have some drop of Irish blood, seeing that nearly half a million Irish immigrants arrived in Australia during the eighteen hundreds.

During the nineteen century there was a great need for tradesmen and labourers in the colonies and assisted passage was offered to Irish people who were willing to emigrate there. Therefore with the failure of Ireland's stable food, the "Humble Spud" or potato , many an Irish family took advantage of this assistance. On arrival at the port of entry in most cases the following details were recorded:- name, age, occupation, religion, level of literacy, place of origin, parents' names, and in some cases, the maiden name of the mother is given. All of this is very important when referring to the Parish records in Ireland. All this information is available in the New South Wales Archives , where one can refer to the Guide to Shipping and the Free Passenger lists. The staff of these Archives are very helpful.

In the Public Records Office in Victoria and the City Reference Office Melbourne, you will find copies of the records of unassisted as well as assisted immigrants.

Now in the case of the convict there is so much information available, that in most cases it is relatively easy to get their roots. In the case of the girl who was deported for stealing the bedspread, there was so much information on her convict papers, all that had to be done was contact the Parish Priest in her Parish in Ireland to trace her living relatives. The newspapers in that particular county for that year was referred to and there was a very full account of her trial and sentence. But in other cases there appears to be no record of papers. Perhaps they may have been mislaid or maybe they were never recorded in the first place. The information on this case was available in the Archives Office of Tasmania. On the record papers was such information as name, the name of the ship she travelled in, the date she arrived in Tasmania and the port she arrived at. Also included was; her age, where in Ireland her trial took place, a discription of her offence and also her sentence.

A record of convict ships and their cargoes arriving at Sydney are to be found in the New South Wales Archives in Sydney. A more complete account of these records will be found in Guide to the Convict Record in the Archives office.

In quite a number of cases some convicts, of good conduct, had their wives and children sent out to join them and having been granted their freedom made a new life for themselves in the new country. In some cases it is said that some convicts liked the new country so much that on their release, having returned to Ireland, they again committed a crime so that they would be tried and transported again.

Australia would appear to be much like Ireland, when it comes to records of births, marriages and deaths. Records appear to vary from state to state. Civil registration began in Southern Australia 1843, Victoria 1854, and New South Wales 1857. Death Certificates in some states give quite a lot of information. Some give the birthplace of the deceased. In the case of Marriage Certificates many, as well as giving the birthplace of the person concerned, also give the parents' names, in some cases the maiden name of the mother, and even the occupation of the father. This information is really of great value when one is bridging the gap between the new country and the homeland.

The records in New South Wales for the period, from 1788 to 1899, that is of births, marriages and deaths are available for inspection on micro-film in the Sydney Archives Office. A visit is really something that is well worth the time and effort and many people have been very happy with information self-researched here.

It all sounds like, and is, hard work, but people who have gone to this kind of trouble in doing their homework, find it well worth the effort when they have all the information compiled together at home before following it up in Ireland.

As said earlier if you have tried all the other sources and still have not come up with any link between your country and the homeland, you can now resort to your letter to one of the Irish Provincial Newspapers. Most Irish homes get a copy of their own county or district newspaper. Below is a list of these and all you need do is address your letter to the editor of the particular paper. Included also is the name of the town where published.

County	Name of Newspaper and where Published	
Antrim	Belfast Newsletter	Belfast
Armagh	The Guardian	Armagh
Carlow	The Leinster Times	Carlow
Cavan	The Anglo Celt	Cavan
Clare	The Clare Champion	Ennis
Cork	The Cork Examiner	Cork

Derry	The Derry Journal	Derry
Donegal	The Donegal Democrat	Ballyshannon
Down	The Leader	Dromore
Dublin	The Irish Press	Dublin
	The Irish Independent	Dublin
	The Irish Times	Dublin
Fermanagh	Impartial Reporter	Enniskillen
Galway	The Connaught Tribune	Galway
Kerry	The Kerryman	Tralee
Kildare	The Leinster Leader	Naas
Kilkenny	Kilkeeny People	Kilkenny
Laois	The Leinster Express	Portlaoise
Leitrim	The Leitrim Observer	Carrick-on-Shannon
Limerick	The Limerick Leader	Limerick
Longford	The Longford Leader	Longford
Louth	Dundalk Democrat	Dundalk
Mayo	The Western People	Ballina
Monaghan	The Monaghan Argus	Monaghan
Offaly	The Midland Tribune	Birr
Roscommon	The Roscommon Herald	Boyle
Sligo	The Sligo Champion	Sligo
Tipperary	The Tipperary Star	Thurles
Tyrone	The Dungannon Observer	Dungannon
Waterford	The Munster Express	Waterford
Westmeath	The Westmeath Examiner	Mullingar
Wexford	The Free Press	Wexford
Wicklow	The Wicklow People	Wicklow

The list above should be of great value to you, and will probably get many an answer to your letter. In some places there are other newspapers as well, but they are less useful for the purpose required. You should be able to figure out, from the Christian names referred to, in the replies you will receive, if they are of the same family as yours. As stated earlier the same Christian names will probably appear over and over again in the one family, especially if the name of your ancestor is unusual, but it may be added that a name like Patrick, will appear in most Irish families. But anyway it is well worth a try and you will probably enjoy some of the answers you will get, and many a friendship has begun this way.

ARRIVING "HOME"
(TO IRELAND)

By now you will have gathered all the information available to you in your own country, you may even have already got in contact with your Irish relations, using the information you have pieced together already.

Converselly if you have not yet located or found out anything about any of your Irish relations, it is time for you to have your vacation in Ireland. It is worth mentioning here, that people in Ireland nearly always use the term "Coming Home" when they meet third or even fourth generation Irish, even if they never previously stood on Irish soil. Someone is nearly always bound to ask the question, When did you come 'Home'? In many cases the visitor is amused by this but such a question should certainly make you feel welcome.

Even if you do not "come home" you can, by mail, avail of much information by just writing to some of the places I will mention later on. Now assuming you have arrived in Ireland, complete with all your notes. Well where do you start? To begin with, if you are tracing somebody who was born after 1864 and you are sure which county your ancestor was born in, but you have not got the correct townland, you could start by paying a visit to the office of records in that particular county, that is, the records of births, marriages and deaths. You will find these addresses and telephone numbers in any Irish telephone directory. You can give what details you have, approximate date of birth, parents' names, also names of brothers and sisters your ancestor may have had as this will give the registrar something to go on. There will be many different districts in each county, so you may have to leave it with him for at least a couple of days. If the surname is not very common to the county you may be lucky enough, that is, if the registrar is not too busy, to get the required information quickly. Of course if you know the townland the record may be looked up while you are there. In fact this is some work you could have done at home, by writing. The records in these offices may not be inspected by yourself as their contents are confidential, but when the correct entry is found you may obtain a copy of it.

Some people continue their search here if the entry they are looking for is found. From this they will have the ancestor's parents' names, also the maiden name of the mother, so it will be easy to find other children that may have been born to the same parents. By doing this you will be in a position to find out what happened to the others, because their marriages and deaths will probably also be registered here, that is, if they did not emigrate or move to a different county. By doing this also you can find out, if they had children born of the marriage. Again you may find, if these children married and had their own children. It sounds confusing, but the generation you have come to by now would probably be of your own generation. So from this you may find out if you still have some living relatives in Ireland.

On the birth certificates you will get the following information. Father's full name, maiden name of mother, sponsors, occupation of father, as well of course, date of birth, and by whom the birth was registered. In the case of a marriage, the Christian name of the groom's father, the Christian name of the bride's father, the occupation of both fathers, the occupations of the bride and groom, as well as their ages, where they got married and where they resided at the time of the marriage. Also the sponsors, who were nearly always close family or in some cases very close neighbours is usually recorded. With death Certificates, the name of the deceased, his age, where he died and the name of spouse if still living, what the person died from, and by whom the death was registered.

One must remember that some of ones ancestors

An Irish Cabin   (Courtesy of the National Library)

could have died in the State workhouses which were established at that time, so if you do not find the death entry you are looking for, you should not forget to look up these records. They are kept in separate books. The registrar will advise you on this. You will find the staff of these offices very helpful. But you must also remember that very many deaths at this time were never recorded, possibly because of the illiteracy.

Now from here you can pay a visit to the Parish Priest of the Parish you are interested in. Of course if you have the name of the Parish in the first place there is no need to go to the office of the County or City Registrar. You will also find most of the Clergy very helpful. They are well used to dealing with such queries. In many parishes the old records have been rewritten from the original Latin ones, and these are well indexed so with very little effort the entry may be looked up. On finding the correct entry the Priest will usually refer back to the original entry, just to make sure he has the correct one, and in some cases there may be little notes added. This will happen in cases where the baptised person would have got married in a different Parish. He would have contacted his own Parish for his baptismal Certificate. In such a case there would be a little note added to the baptism entry, stating details of the marriage. While here you can also get details of other family members.

The records here will give somewhat much the same information as the State Records; the name of the townland will be included, and of course the parents' names but not their occupations.

While you are here you may want to visit the Church itself, where your ancestors would have been baptised, married and would have rested for the last night before being buried in the local Churchyard (Cemetery). The local Churchyard will more than likely be near the Church itself. In some cases where the Church is relatively new, the Churchyard will most likely be found at the site of the old Parish Church. It is not unusual to find an almost forgotten Churchyard in a remote place, some distance from the road. In these you will find some quite noble headstones, some showing three or four generations of certain families. It can be a great and peaceful experience to just browse and read some of the inscriptions.

While in Ireland you should try to meet some of the older inhabitants of the area. It may well surprise you all the information they may be able to give you as unusual stories about different families will have been handed down from generation to generation, and it is a well known fact that Irish people love to talk. When paying such a visit to the local Churchyard, it is advisable to bring with you a notebook and pencil, some chalk, a pocket knife an old cloth and some brown paper. Some of the stones may have a thick coating of ivy and moss, try to remove this by hand with the help of the knife, on no account use a wire brush as this will damage the stone. When the coating is removed from the stone rub it with some ordinary chalk this will enable you to read the inscription. You may also lay a sheet of brown paper on the stone rub with a pencil by doing this you can get the inscription to transfer onto the paper. In some cases where the stone is not too moss covered, just rub it hard with some wet grass and this will enable you to read the inscription more clearly.

While Irish cemeteries have some very fine and noble stones, some graves are marked with a Cross and no inscription, and sad to say there are many unmarked graves especially from the Famine years when thousands of Irish people young and old went to early graves. So bear these poor souls in mind and say a little prayer for them while you are browsing around.

Here lyeth the body
of John Hure who depd
Life April ye 17th 1794
Agd 47 yrs & his daughter
Margaret died
July ye 28th 1796 agd 15 yrs
and also his sister
Mary Hure died S'ber
ye 12 1796 agd 30 yrs
R.I.P.

Inscription on tombstone, at Tankardstown Churchyard County Limerick.

Many a visitor to Ireland find it very interesting to pay a visit to the old National school which an ancestor may have attended. With the assistance of the head master, it can be interesting to look through the old roll books.

The Old National School, Bruree, County Limerick, attended by Eamonn de Valera now it is a museum called after him.

EAMONN DE VALERA 1882-1975

Eamonn de Valera, born in New York 1882. He came to Ireland as a child, to live with his uncle in County Limerick. He joined the volunteers before 1916 and took an active part in the Easter week rising. Following the surrender, he was sentenced to death. This sentence was commuted to penal servitude for life. He founded the Fianna Fáil party, and entered Dail Eireann in 1927. In 1932 he became head of government and as leader of his party won many subsequent general elections. He became President of Ireland in 1959. Died in 1975.

[B.O. 3

Page 1

N.B.—In writing out this Roll keep the Names of the Pupils of same class, as far as possible, on same page. Place the names of the Paid Monitors to be examined for Results after names of the ordinary pupils of the class in which they are to be examined.

After having made the necessary notings from this Roll, as to pupils eligible for promotion, Teacher is requested to send it immediately to the Education Office where full details of the marks obtained by the pupils examined will be inserted for the information of the Manager and the Teacher.

188*9*

District No. *52*

Roll No. *8572*

P. L. Union. *Kilmallo—*

County. *Limerick*

Bruce Male National School.

Name and Address of Manager, *Revᵈ E. Sheehy P.P. Bruree*

Post Town of School, *Brur—*

EXAMINATION ROLL

(AND PROMOTION SHEET)

Of all Pupils whose Names were on the Rolls on the last day of Month preceding Examination, and w made 100 or more Attendances within the previous year. (12 Months.)

Year ended *30—* day of *June* 188*9*—(Last day of Month preceding Examination.)

Dated, *25ᵗʰ July 1889* Signed, *John Kelly* Teacher.

Register No.	Names of Pupils in the order of Classes as permitted for Examination with the lowest class. (Enter the names of Pupils examined previously in same class first in order)	Age last Birthday.	No. of Attendances made in Year.	In what Class (lowest in School)	On what Class last year Attendance			Name and Roll No. H.C.		Reading		Writing		Arithmetic		Spelling		Grammar		Geography				Months each.
									Pass	A.	Pass	A.	Pass	A.	Pass	A.	Pass	A.	Pass	A.				
	Infants																								
419	Pat Horgan	6							✓																
432	Wᵐ Coohy	6							✓																
454	John Daly	5							✓																
426	Michⁱ O'Brien	5							✓																
441	Eddie Donelan	6							✓																
445	Jim Hannan	6					X																		
487	John Savage	5							✓																
429	Frank Ward	5					X																		
440	Thˢ Coleman	5							✓																
443	Pat Carroll	4							✓																
448	John Murphy	4							✓																
452	Gerald Ruddle	4							✓																
453	Jaˢ Coleman	4							✓																
454	John Morrissy	4							✓																

IRISH LIBRARIES
AND
OTHER RECORD OFFICES

To my mind there is no more pleasant place to spend an afternoon than in one of our libraries. Here you can do a lot towards tracing your ancestors.

Let us again assume you have often been told that your ancestor spoke frequently about one particular place but you do not know in which county this place is. Well when you get to one of the larger libraries (these will be in the cities or larger towns) you should look up a book called the Townlands and Towns of Ireland. If there is such a place you will find it in this bok. The book is in alphabetical order, so you will not have much trouble finding it. You may have one small problem. You may find that there are many townlands of the same name but you will be told in which county each one is. But as stated earlier the surname concerned is a good guide to which county you are looking for. If you do come up with the wrong county, you can always telephone the Registrar of the other county to see if they have any record of your ancestor. You should be hopeful if you have the name of the townland even without the name of the county.

Let us now say you have succeeded with the search for both townland and county, but on arriving at this address you are unable to find the family you are looking for. Here again it is a case of back to the library. Assuming you have checked the Parish records and have found you no longer have relatives in the area but of course you are still interested in going to see the cottage or farm where your ancestor was born and reared.

In the early 1850s there was a general valuation of Ire-

Sarsfield St. Kilmallock, Co. Limerick — (Courtesy of the National Library)

32

land done. The purpose of this was to establish a fair rent on property holders. The returns of this valuation filled nearly two hundred volumes, you will find the volume to cover each district in the city library nearest it. Only the Valuation Office in Dublin would house the complete set.

The man responsible for compiling these books was a Dublin geologist named Richard Griffith and hence it is known as Griffith's Valuation. From this valuation one can get such particulars as, the name of each individual property holder, the townland or street, the name of the landlord, a description of the property holding and of course the amount of the valuation assessment. With these particulars and the help of an Ordanance Survey map, you will probably be able to locate the land or house of your ancestor. Failing this if you contact the Irish Valuation Office, Dublin, the staff there will be able to help you, as they will have the records of the transfer of each property from one owner to another, as all transfers had to be registered with the Land Registry Office. So by referring to this source you may be able to trace the name of the present day owner of the land or cottage once owned by your ancestor.

If you want to go back and see if the land belonged to your ancestor before the 1850s, there was another valuation done in the 1820s, the reason for this one was for rent to be paid for the upkeep of the Protestant Church which was the established Church at that time. This survey may suit you even better that is, if your ancestor had left during the early 1800s. You can also trace present day owners, through the Irish Valuation Office. The only difficulty in this case is, that people without land were not recorded. So if your ancestor and his family lived in a village they would not have been recorded.

Again if you are tracing somebody who may have left Ireland around the turn of the century, there was a general census of Ireland in 1901. Each household would have been included in this. In it you will find the following information, the name of the head of the house, also every other person in the house their religion, education, age, occupation, where born and if they were Irish speakers or not.

When one speaks about tracing their ancestors or roots, one if often inclined to think of people who would have left Ireland during the Famine years. It is amazing the number of people whose grandparents may have left Ireland, around the turn of the century and had not kept in touch with home or perhaps the whole family may have left about that time, and their grandchildren have now returned trying to locate the birthplace of the grandparent, or in some cases looking for any relatives who may have stayed at home.

Most people who left Ireland, would have departed from Queenstown, now known as Cobh. It is the port in Cork and there have been many songs and poems written about such partings. It was also the custom of that time to hold a farewell party in the home of the person who would be "Bidding farewell" the following morning. This was known as "The American Wake". All family, friends and relations would gather for the night to say a final good-bye, and to console the heartborken family remaining behind. In many cases, one member of the family would go to the New World and work hard so that they could earn the fare to send back to Ireland so that another member of the family could travel out to join them. Each member in turn would save money to bring the rest of the brothers and sisters to join them. In many cases only the mother and father would remain at home.

ROMAN CATHOLIC DIOCESES

with the Counties, or parts of, within their boundaries

ACHONRY - Parts of Mayo, Sligo, and Roscommon.
ARDAGH & CLONMACNOISE - Most of Longford, parts of Leitrim and Offaly, small parts of Westmeath, Roscommon, Cavan and Sligo.
ARMAGH - Most of Louth & Armagh, parts of Tyrone and Derry and small part of Meath.
CASHEL - Parts of Tipperary and Limerick.
CLOGHER - Monaghan, most of Fermanagh, part of Tyrone and small parts of Donegal, Louth and Cavan.
CLONFERT- Part of Galway and small parts of Roscommon and Offaly.
CLOYNE - Part of Cork County.
CORK & ROSS - Cork City and part of County Cork.
DERRY - Most of Derry, parts of Tyrone and Donegal.
DOWN & CONNOR - Almost the whole of Antrim, part of Down and small part of Derry.
DROMORE - Part of Down and small parts of Armagh and Antrim.
DUBLIN - Almost the whole of Dublin, most of Wicklow, part of Kildare, small parts of Carlow, Wexford and Laois.
ELPHIN - Most of Roscommon, parts of Sligo and Galway.
FERNS - Almost the whole of Wexford and part of Wicklow.
GALWAY - Parts of Galway, Clare and Mayo.
KERRY - Almost the whole of Kerry and small part ot Cork.
KILDARE & LEIGHLIN - Almost the whole of Carlow and parts of Laois, Offaly, Kilkenny, Wicklow, and a small part of Wexford.
KILLALA - Parts of Mayo and Sligo.
KILLALOE - Most of Clare, parts of Tipperary, Offaly, Galway and small parts of Limerick and Laois.
KILMORE - Most of Cavan, parts of Leitrim and Fermanagh, small parts of Meath and Sligo.
LIMERICK - Most of Limerick, parts of Clare and small parts of Kerry.
MEATH - Most of Meath and Westmeath, part of Offaly, and small parts of Cavan, Longford, Louth and Dublin.
OSSORY - Most of Kilkenny, parts of Laois and a small part of Offaly.
RAPHOE - Most of Donegal.
TUAM - Parts of Mayo, Galway and a small part of Roscommon.
WATERFORD & LISMORE - Waterford, part of Tipperary, small part of Cork.
Each of these Dioceses, consists of Parishes from the fifferent Counties mentioned.
   In the next pages is a complete list of Parishes in each county, but as you can see from above that does not mean that a Parish will come under the same Diocese as it does County.

List of Roman Catholic
Parishes

Co. Antrim
Ahoghill
Antrim
Armoy
Ballintoy
Ballyclare
Ballymacarett
Ballymoney &
  Derrykeighan
Belfast City
  St. Malachy
  St. Patrick
  St. Peter
  St. Mary
  St. Joseph
Braid
Carnlough
Carrickfergus
Culfeightrin
Cushendall
Cushendun
Derryaghy
Duneane
Dunloy & Cloughmills
Glenavy & Killead
Glenarm
Greencastle
Kirkinriola
  (Ballymena)
Larne
Loughuile
Portglenone
Portrush
Ramoan (Ballycastle)
Randalstown
Rasharkin
Tickmacrevan
  (Glenarm)

Co. Armagh
Aghagallon & Ballinderry
Armagh
Ballymacnab
Ballymore & Mullaghbrac
  (Tandragee)
Creggan Lower (Cullyhanne)
Creggan Upper
  (Crossmaglen)
Derrynose (Keady)
Drumcree (Portadown)
Forkhill
Killeavy (Bessbrook)
Kilmore

Loughgall
Loughgilly
Lurgan (Shankill)
Seagoe
Tynan

Co. Carlow
Bagenalstown (Muine Bheag)
Ballon
Borris
Carlow
Clonegall
Clonmore
Hacketstown
Leighlinbridge
Myshall
St. Mullins
Tinryland
Tullow

Co. Cavan
Annagh (Belturbet)
Ballintemple
Castlerahan
  (Ballyjamesduff)
Castletera
Crosserlough
Denn
Drumgoon
Drumlane
Drumlumman North
  Swanlinbar
Kilbridge &
Mountnugent
Killann (Ballieboro')
Killinkere
Killeshandra
Kilmore
Kilsherdany and Drung
Kinawley
Kingscourt
Knockbride
Laragh
Lavey
Lurgan
Templeport
Urney & Anaghellif

Co. Clare
Ballina
Ballyvaughan
Broadford
Carron

36

O'Callaghan's Mills
Carrigaholt
Clareabbey
Clondegad
Clonrush
Corofin
Cratloe
Crusheen
Doonass & Trugh
Doora & Kilraghtis
Dysart
Ennis
Ennistymon
Feakle Lr.
Inagh
Inch & Kilmaley
Kilballyowen
Kildysart
Kilfarboy
Kilfenora
Kilfidane
Kilkee
Kilkeedy
Killaloe
Killanena
Killard
Killimar
Kilmacduane
Kilmihil
Kilmurray-Ibricane (Mullagh)
Kilmurry-McMahon
Kilnoe &
　Tuamgraney
Kilrush
Liscannor
Lisdoonvarna
Newmarket-on-Fergus
New Quay
Ogonnelloe
Parteen
Quin
Scariff & Moynoe
Sixmilebridge
Tulla

Co. Cork
Aghabulloge
Aghada
Aghinagh
Annakissy
Ardfield & Rathbarry
Aughadown
Ballincollig
Ballnhassig
Ballyclough
Ballyhea

Ballymacoda &
　Lady's Bridge
Ballyvourney
Bandon
Bantry
Blackrock
Blarney
Boherbue
Bonane
Barryroe
Buttevant
Caheragh
Carrigaline
Carrigtwohill
Castlemagner
Castlelyons
Castletownroche
Charleville or Rathluirc
Clondrohid
Clonmeen
Clonthead &
　Ballingeary
Cloyne
Cobh
Conna
Cork City
　St. Finbarr
　St. Patrick
　St. Peter & Paul
　St. Mary
Courceys
Castletownbere
Castlehaven
Clonakilty &
　Darrara
Donaghmore
Doneraile
Douglas
Drimoleague
Dromtariffe
Dunmanway
Enniskeane &
　Desertserges
Eyeries
Fermoy
Freemount
Glanmire
Glanworth &
　Ballindangan
Glounthane
Goleen
Grenagh
Imogeely
Inniscarra
Innishannon
Iveleary

Kanturk
Kilbehenny
Kilbritain
Kildorrery
Killeagh
Kilmichael
Kilnamartyra
Kilmurry
Kilworth
Kilmeen &
   Castleventry
Kinsale
Liscarrol
Lisgoold
Macroom
Mallow
Midleton
Millstreet
Mitchelstown
Monkstown
Mourne Abbey
Muintervara
Murragh
Newmarket
Ovens
Passage
Rath & Islands
Rathcormac
Rathmore
Roscarberry &
   Lissevard
Schull
Shandrum
Skibbereen
Timoleague &
   cloghagh
Tracton Abbey
Watergrasshill
Youghal

Co. Derry
Ballinderry
Ballynascreen
Ballyscullion
   (Bellaghy)
Banagher
Coleraine
Cumber Upr. Learmount
   (Claudy)
Desertmartin
Drumehose
   (Limavady)
Dungiven
Errigal
Faughanvale

Glendermot
   (Waterside)
Kilrea
Magilligan
Maghera
Magherafelt
Moneymore
Templemore
   (Derry City)
Termoneeny

Co. Donegal
All Saints, Killea &
   Taugh-Boyne
   (St. Johnston)
Annagry
Aughnish and Aughaninshin
   (Ramelton)
Castlemacaward &
   Templecrone (Dungloe)
Clondahorky (Dunfanaghy)
Conwal & Lech
   (Letterkenny)
Drumhome
Glencolumkille
Gweedore
Iniskeel (Glenties)
Inver
Kilcar
Killybegs &
   Killaghtee
Killygarvan &
   Tullyfern
Killymard
Kilbarron
   (Ballyshannon)
Kilmacrenan
Kilteevogue
Mevagh (Carrigart)
Raphoe
Stranorlar
Termin & Gartan
Tullybegley East,
   Raymunterdoney &
   Tory
Burt, Inch & Fahan
Clonca (Malin)
Clonleigh (Lifford)
Clonmany
Culdaff
Desertegny &
   Lower Fahan (Buncrana)
Donagh (Carndonagh)
Donaghmore
Iskaheen &
   Moville Upper
Moville Lower

Co. Down
Aghaderg
  (Loughbrickland)
Annaclone
Ardkeen
Ballygalget
  (Portaferry)
Ballynahinch
Banbridge
Ballyphilip
Bangor
Bright (Ardglass)
Clonallon
  (Warrenpoint)
Clonduff (Hilltown)
Donaghmore
Dromara
Drumaroad
  (Castlewellan)
Drumbo, Drumgath
  (Rathfriland)
Drumgooland Upr.
Drumgooland Lr.
Downpatrick
Dunsford
Kilbroney
  (Rostrevor)
Kilclief &
  Strangford
Kilcoo (Rathfriland)
Kilkeel
Loughinisland
Maghera &
  Bryansford
  (Newcastle)
Magheralin
Moira
Mourne
Newcastle
Newry
Newtownards, Comber,
  & Donaghadee
Saintfield
  (Downpatrick)
Saul & Ballee
Tullylish
Tyrella & Dundrum

Co. Dublin
Balbriggan
Baldoyle
Balrothery
Blanchardstown
Booterstown
Clondalkin
Donabate

Dublin City
St. Aghatha
  (Nr. William Street)
St. Andrew
  (Westland Row)
St, Audeon
  (High Street)
St. Catherine
  (Meath Street)
St. James
  (James Street)
.St. Laurence O'Toole
  (Seville Place)
St. Mary
  (Pro-Cathedral,
  Marlborough Street)
St. Michael & John
  (Lr. Exchange Street)
St. Michan
  (Halston Street)
St. Nicholas of Myra
  (Francis Street)
St. Paul
  (Arran Quay)
Dun Laoire

Finglas
Garristown
Howth
Lucan
Lusk
Palmerstown
Rathfarnham
Rolestown
Saggart
Sandyford
Skerries
Swords

Co. Fermanagh
Aghavea
Aughalurcher
  (Lisnaskea)
Carn (Belleek)
Cleenish
Culmaine
Devenish
Enniskillen
Galloon
Inishmacsaint
Irvinestown
Roslea
Tempo

Co. Galway
Abbeyknockmoy

Addergoole
Liskeevy
Annaghdown
Aran Islands
Athenry
Ahascragh
Ardarahan
Abbeygormican &
  Killoran
Augrim &
  Kilconnell
Ballymacward &
  Clonkeenkerrill
Ballinakill
Ballaun, Grange &
  Killaan
Beagh
Ballinakill
Boyounagh
Creagh & Kilcloney
  (Ballinasloe)
Clonfert, Donanaghta,
  & Meelick
Clontuskert
Claregalway
Castlegar
Duniry & Kilnelahan
Donaghpatrick &
  Kilcoona
Dunmore
Fahy & Kilquain
Fohenagh &
  Kilgerrill
Galway-St. Nicholas
Kilconickny,
Kilconieran &
  Lickerrig
Kilcooley & Leitrim
Killalaghten &
  Kilrickhill
Killimorbologue &
  Tiranascragh
Killimordaly &
  Kiltullagh
Kilmalinoge &
  Lickmolassy
  (Portumna)
Kilnadeema
Kiltomer & Oghill
Killian & Killeroran
  (Ballygar)
Kilcummin
  (Oughterard)
Killannin
Kilcameen &
  Ballynacourty

Kinvarra
Kilbeacanty
Kilchreest
Kilcolgan,
Killeenavara &
  Dromacoo
Kilcornan
Killora &
  Killogilleen
Kilmacduagh &
  Kiltartan
Kilthomas
Kilkerrin &
  Clonberne
Killascobe
Killeen (Carroroe)
Killererin
Kilmoylan & Cummer
Loughrea
Lettermore
Lackagh
Moycullen
Moylough &
  Mountbellow
Moyrus
Oranmore
Omey & Ballindoon
Rahoon
Roundstone
Salthill
Spiddal
Tynagh
Tuam
Woodford

Co. Kerry
Abbeydorney
Annascaul
Ardfert
Ballinskelligs
Ballybunion
Ballyferritor
Ballyheigue
Ballylongford
Ballymacelligott
Boherbue
Bonane &
  Glengariffe
Brosna
Cahiceiveen
Cahirdaniel
Castlegregory
Castleisland
Castlemaine
Causeway
Dingle

Dromod
Duagh
Firies
Fossa
Glenbeigh
Glenflesk
Kenmare
Kilcummin
Kilgarvan
Killarney
Killeentierna
Killorglin
Knocknagoshel
Listowel
Lixnaw
Milltown
Moyvane
Prior
Rathmore
Sneem
Spa
Tarbert
Tralee
Tuogh
Tuosist
Valentia

Co. Kildare
Allen
Athy
Ballymore Eustace
Balyna (Johnstown)
Caragh (Downings)
Carbury
Castledermot
Celbridge
Clane
Clonbullogue
Kilcock
Kilcullen
Kildare
Kill
Maynooth
Monasterevin
Naas
Narraghmore
Newbridge
Suncroft

Co. Kilkenny
Aghaviller
Ballyhale
Ballyregget
Callan
Castlecomer
Clara

Clough
Conahy
Danesforth
Dunnemaggan
Durrow
Freshford
Galmory
Glenmore
Gowran
Graignenamanagh
Inistiogue
Johnstown
Kilmacow
Lisdowney
Mooncoin
Muckalee
Mullinavat
Paulstown
Rosbercon
St. Canice's
   (Kilkenny)
St. John's
   (Kilkenny)
St. Mary's
   (Kilkenny)
St. Patrick's
   (Kilkenny)
Slieverue
Templeorum
Thomastown
Tullaherin
Tulleroan
Urlingford
Windgap

Co. Laois
Abbeyleix
Aghaboe
Arles
Ballinakill
Ballyadams
Ballyfin
Borris-in-Ossory
Camross (Mountrath)
Castletown
Clonaslee
Durrow
Mountmellick
Mountrath
Portarlington
Portlaoise
Raheen
Rathdowney
Rosenallis
Stradbally

41

Co. Leitrim
Annaduff
Aughavas
Ballinamore
Ballymeehan
  (Rossinver)
Carrigallen
Clooneclare
  (Manorhamilton)
Drumlease
  (Dromahaire)
Drumreilly
Fenagh
Glenade
Gortletheragh
Inishmagrath
  (Drumkeeran)
Killargue
Killasnet
Killenummery &
  Killerny
Kiltoghert
Kiltubbrid
Kinlough
Mohill-Manachain

Co. Limerick
Abbeyfeale
Adare
Ardagh
Ardpatrick
Askeaton
Athea
Ballingarry
Ballybricken
Ballygran &
  Colman's Well
Ballylanders
Banogue
Bruff
Bulgaden &
  Ballinvana
Caherconlish
Cappagh
Cappamore
Castleconnell
Coolcappa
Cola & Solohead
Croagh
Croom
Donaghmore
Doon
Dromin - Athlacca
Drumcollogher
Effin
Emly

Fedamore
Feenagh
Galbally
Glenroe
Glin
Hospital
Kilbehenny
Kildimo
Kilfinane
Killeedy
Kilmallock-Ballingaddy
Kilteely
Knockaderry
Knockaney
Knocklong
Loughill
Mahoonagh **or**
Castlemahon
Manister
Monagea
Mungret
Murroe & Boher
Newcastle West
Pallasgreen
Parteen
Patrickswell
Rathkeale
Rockhill & Bruree
Shanagolden & Foynes
Stonehall
Templeglantine
Tournafulla
Limerick City
  St. John's
  St. Joseph's
  St. Mary's
  St. Michael's
  St. Munchin's
  St. Patrick's
  St. Paul's

Co. Longford
Abbeylara
Ardagh
Carrickedmond
Cashel
Clonbroney
Clonguish
Columcille
  (Dring)
Drumlish
Granard
Kilcommuck
Kilglass
Killashee
Killoe
Mostrim

42

Moydow
Rathcline
Scabby
 (Cloonagh)
Shrule
 (Ballymahon)

Co. Louth
Ardee
Carlingford
Clogherhead
Collon
Darver
Dundalk
Dunleer
Faughart
Kilkerley
Kilsaran
Lordship &
 Ballymascanlan
Louth
Mellifont
Monasterboice
Drogheda
St. Mary's
St. Peter's
Talanstown
Termonfeckin
Togher

Co. Mayo
Attymas
Addergoole
Ardagh
Aughaval
 (Westport)
Achill
Aghamore
Aglish, Ballyheane
 & Breaghwy
 (Castlebar)
Aghagower
 (Westport)
Bohola
Backs (Rathduff)
Ballycastle
Ballysokeary
Belmullet
Bally & Manilla
Ballinrobe
Ballyovey
Bekan (Claremorris)
Burriscarra &
 Ballintubber
 (Claremorris)
Burrishoole

 (Newport)
Ballyhaunis
Crossmolina
Clare Island
Cong & Neale
Crossboyne &
 Tagheen
Clonbur
Islandeady
 (Castlebar)
Kilconduff &
 Meelick (Swinford)
Kilgarvan (Ballina)
Killaser (Swinford)
Kilbeagh
 (Charlestown)
Killedan
Killmovee
Kilshalvey
Kilfian
Killala
Kilmoremoy
 (Ballina)
Kiltane
 (Bangor-Erris)
Keelogues
Kilcolman
 (Claremorris)
Kilcommon &
 Robeen
Kilgeever
 (Louisburg)
Kilmaine
Kilmeena
Knock
Kilbride
Lackan
Moyo & Roslee
Templemore
Toomore (Foxford)
Turlough (Castlebar)

Co. Meath
Ardcath
Athboy
Ballinabrackey
Ballinvor &
 Kildalkey
Beauparc
 (Yellow Furze)
Blacklion
Bohermeen (Navan)
Carnaross
Castletown (Navan)
Clonmellon
Curragh (Ashbourne)

Drumconrath
Duleek
Dunboyne
Dunderry
Dunshaughlin
Johnstown
Kells
Kilbride
Kilmainham &
  Moybologue
Kilcoon (Dunboyne)
Kilbeg (Kells)
Kilmessan & Dunsay,
Kilskyre
  (Ballinlough)
Lobinstown (Navan)
Longwood
Moynalty
Navan
Nobber
Oldcastle
Oristown (Kells)
Rathkenny
Ratoath & Ashbourne
Rosnaree & Donore
Skyrne
stamullen
Summerhill
Trim

Co. Monaghan
Aghabog
Aughmullen
Clontibret
Clones
Donagh (Glasslough)
·Donaghmoyne
Drumully (Scotshouse)
Drumsnat & Kilmore
Ematris (Rockcorry)
Errigal Trough
  (Emyvale)
Killevin (Newbliss)
Monaghan
Maghaire Rois
Magheracloone
  (Carrickmacross)
Muckno (Castleblaney
Tullycorbet
  (Ballybay)
Tydavnet

Co. Offaly
Birr
Clara
Clonmacnoise

Daingean
Dunkerrin
Edenderry
Eglish
Gallen & Reynagh
  (Banagher)
Kilcormac
Killeigh (Geashill)
Killina (Rahan)
Kinnetty
Lemanaghan
  (Ferbane)
Lusmagh
Rhode
Siernieran
Shinrone
Tisaran & Fuithre
  (Ferbane)
Tullamore

Co. Roscommon
Ardcarne
Athleague & Fuerty
Aughrim & Kilmore
Ballintober
  (Ballymoe)
Boyle & Kilbryan
Castlemore &
  Kilcolman
Cloontuskert,
Kilgeffin
Dysert & Tissara
Elphin & Creeve
Glinsk & Kilbegnet
Kilbride
Kilcorkey &
  Frenchpark
Kilglass & Rooskey
Killeevan (Castlerea)
Killukin
Kilnamanagh &
  Estersnow
Kiltoom
Kiltrustan,
Lissonnuffy &
  Cloonfinlough
  (Strokestown)
Loughglynn
Ogulla & Baslick
Oran
Roscommon & Kilteevan
St. John's
  (Knockcroghery)
Tibohine

44

Co. Sligo
Aghanagh (Ballinafad)
Ahamlish (Cliffoney)
Ballisodare
Killvarett
Cloonacool
Curry
Drumcliffe
Drumrat
Easky
Emelfad & Kilmorgan
Geevagh
Kilfree & Killaraght
Killoran
Kilmacteigue
Kilshalvey & Kilturra
  & Cloonoghill
Riverstown
Skreen & Dromard
Sligo, Coolera, Calry
Rosses Point &
  St. Mary's
Templeboy
Tumore

Co. Tipperary
Annacarty
Ardfinnan
Ballinahinch
Ballingarry
Ballylooby
Ballyneale
Ballyporeen
Bansha & Kilmoyler
Boherlahan & Dulla
Borrisokane
Borrisoleigh
Burgess & Youghal
Cahir
Carriskp-on-Suir
Cashel
Castletownnarrha
Clerihan
Clogheen
Cloghprior & Monsea
Clonmel
Clonoulty
Cloughjordan
Cappawhite
Drangan
Drom & Inch
Dunkerrin
Emly
Fethard & Killusty
Golden
Gortnahoe

Holycross
Kilbarron
Kilcommon
Killenaule
Kilsheelan
Knockavilla
Lattin & Cullen
Loughmore
Moycarky
Mullinahone
Nenagh
Newcastle
New Inn
Newport
Oola & Solohead
Powerstown
Roscrea
Silvermines
Templemore
Templetuohy
Thurles
Toomevarra
Tipperary
Upperchurch

Co. Tyrone
Aghaloo
Ardboe
Ardstraw (Cappagh)
Artrea
Ballinderry
  (Cookstown)
Ballyclog
Beragh
Badoney
Camus (Strabane)
Cappagh
Clogher
Clonfeacle (Moy)
Clonoe (Coalisland)
Desertcreat
Donaghcavey
  (Fintona)
Donaghedy
Donaghenry
  Coalisland
Donaghmore
Dromore
Drumglass
  (Dungannon)
Drumragh (Omagh)
Eglish (Dungannon)
Errigal Keeran
  (Ballygawley)
Killdress

45

Kileeshil
(Tullyallen)
Kilskerry (Trillick)
Leckpatrick
(Strabane)
Lissan (Cookstown)
Longfield
Pomeroy
Termonamongan
Termonmaguirk
(Carrickmore)
Urney

Co. Waterford
Abbeyside
Aglish
Ardmore
Ballyduff
Cappoquin
Carrickbeg
Clashmore
Dungarvan
Dunhill
Kilgobnet
Kill
Killea
Kilrossanty
Kilsheelin
Knockanore
Lismore
Modelligo
Newcastle
Portlaw
Ring
Waterford City
St. John's
St. Patrick's
St. Peter and Paul's
Tallow
Touraneena
Tramore
Trinity Within
Waterford
Trinity Without
Waterford

Co. Westmeath
Ballinacargy
Ballymoe
Castlepollard
Castletown
Clara
Clonmellon
Collinstown
Delvin
Drumraney

Kilbeggan
Kilbridge
Kilkenny West
Killucan
Kinnegad
Lenanaghan&
Ballynahowen
Milltown
Moate & Colry
Moyvore
Mullingar
Multyfarnham
Rathaspick &
Russagh
Rochfortbridge
St. Mary's
(Athlone)
Streete
Taghmon
Tubber
Tullamore
Turbotstown

Co. Wexford
Adamstown
Ballindaggin
Ballygarrett
Ballyoughter
Bennow
Blackwater
Bree
Bunclody
Castlebridge
Clongen
Cloughbawn
Craanford
Crossebeg
Cushinstown
Davidstown
Enniscorthy
Ferns
Glynn
Gorey
Kilanieran
Killaveny
Kilmore
Kilrush
Lady's-Island
Litter
Marshallstown
Mayglass
Monageer
New Ross
Oulart
Oylegate
Piercestown

Ramsgrange
Rathengan
Rathnure
Suttons
Taghmon
Tagoat
Tintern
Templetown
Wexford

Co. Wicklow
Arklow
Ashford

Avoca
Baltinglass
Blessington
Bray Town
Dunlavin
Enniskerry
Glendalough
Kilbride &
 Barnderrig
Kilquade
Rathdrum
Rathvilly
Valleymount
Tinahealy
Wicklow

Church of Ireland or Protestant Parishes

Co. Antrim
Aghalee
Ahogill
Antrim
Ardclinis
Ardoyne
 (Belfast)
Armoy
Ballinderry
Ballintoy
Ballycastle
Ballyclog
Ballyclug
Ballyeaston
Ballymacarrett
 (St. Christopher)
Ballymacarrett
 (Belfast)
Ballymena
Ballymoney
Ballynefeigh
Ballyscullion
Ballysillian
 (Belfast)
Belvior
 (Belfast)
Billy
Broomhedge
Broomfield
Bushmills
Carnmoney
Carrickfergus
Culfeightrin
Christ Church
 (Belfast)

Christ Chruch Cathedral
 (Lisburn)
Cloughfern
Connor
Craigs
Cregagh
 (Belfast)
Cushendun
Derriaghy
Derrykeighan
Derryvolgie
Derrygore
Drummaul
Dunaghy
dundela
 (St. Mark's Belfast)
Dunluce
Dunmury
Dunseverick
Falls Upper
Gartee
Gilnahirk
 (Belfast)
Glenavy
Glynn
Holy Trinity
 (Belfast)
Jordanstown
Kilbride
Killough
Kilmakee
Kilmore
Kilroot
Kirkinriola
Knockbreda
 (Belfast)
Knock Columbkille
 (Belfast)

47

Knocknagoney
  (Belfast)
Laganbank
Lambeg
Larne
Layde
Lisburn
Lurgan
Magdelan
  (Belfast)
Magheragall
Malone
  (Belfast)
Marines
  (Belfast)
Monkstown
Mossley
Mountmerrion
  (Belfast)
Muckamore
Newtowncrommelin
Newtownhamilton
Omeath
Orangefield
Portadown
Portglenone
Portrush
Randalstown
Raskarkin
Rathlin

BELFAST Parishes
Ressurrection
  St. Aidans
  St. Andrews
  St. Annes
  St. Barnabas
  St. Bartholomews
  St. Brendans
  St. Christophers
  St. Clements
  St. Donards
  St. Georges
  St. Jame's
  St. John's
  St. Katherine's
  St. Luke's
  St. Mark's
  St. Mary Madalene's
  St. Matthew's
  St. Matthew's
    (Lisburn)
  St. Matthias's
  St. Nicholas's
  St. Ninnians
  St. Paul's

  St. Peter's
  St. Philip's
  St. Saviour's
  St. Silas's
  St. Simon's
  St. Stephen's
  St. Thomas's
Skerry East
Stormont
  (Belfast)
Templepatrick
Trinity Church
  (Belfast)
Whitehead
Whitehouse
Whiterock
  (Belfast)
Willowfield
  (Belfast)

Co. Armagh
Acton
Annamore
Ardmore
Armagh
armaghbreague
Ballymore
Ballymoyer
Baronstown
Brantry
Carlingford
Carrick
Charlestown
Charlemont
Clare
Clonfeacle
Clonmore
Creggan
Drum
Drumbanagher
Drumcree
Garvagh
Killylea
Kilmore
Knocknamuckley
Lisnadill
Loughagall
Maghera
Middletown
Mullavilly
Richill
St. Savours
Seagoe
Tamlaght
Tandragee
Tullyallen

Tynan

Co. Carlow
Aghade
Aghold
Bagenalstown
Borris
Carlow
Cloydagh
Dunleckney
Fenagh
Hackestown
Lorum
Myshall
Nurney
Painstown
Rathvilly
Staplestown
Tullow
Urglin

Co. Cavan
Annageliffe
Arvagh
Bailieborough
Ballintemple
Ballygamesduff
Ballymachugh
Belturbet
Billis
Castlerahan
Castleterra
Cavan
Cloverhill
Denn
Dernakesk
Derryheen
Derrylane
Drumcar
Drumgoon
Drumlane
Drung
Ematris
Galloon
Kildallon
Killeshandra
Killoughter
Kilmore
Knockbride
Loughan
Quivvy
Shercock
Swanlinbar
Urley
Virginia

Co. Clare
Ballingarry
Ballysumaghan
Clareabbey
Clonlara
Clonlea
Drumcliffe
Ennis
Ennistymon
Feacle
Inishcaltra
Kilbarron
Kildysart
Kilfarboy
Kilfenora
Kilfieragh
Kilfinaghty
Kilkee
Kilkishen
Kilaloe
Killard
Kilmaley
Kilmore
Kilmurry
Kilnasoolagh
Kilrush
Kilsiely
Kyle
Lisdoonvarna
Miltown-Malbay
New Quoy
O'Brien's Bridge
Ogonelloe
Quin
Sellerna
Sixmilebridge
Shannon
Toomgraney

Co. Cork
Abbeystrowry
Adrigole
Aghabullog
  (Coachford)
Aghada
Aghadoe
Aghadown
Aghern
Aglish
Ardagh
Ardfield
Ardghehane
Ardgroom
Ardmore
Ardgeehy
Athnowen

Ballinaboy
Ballinadee
Ballinean
Ballyclough
Ballycotton
Ballydehob
Ballyfeard
Ballyhea
Ballyhooly
Ballymartle
Ballymodan
Ballymoney
Ballynoe
Ballyvourney
Berehaven
Blackrock
   (St. Michael's)
Blarney
Brigown
Brinny
Buttevant
Caheragh
Cannaway
Carrigadrohed
Carrigaline
Carrigamleary
Carrigrohane
Carrigtwohill
Castlehaven
Castlehyde
Castlemacadam
Casltemartyr
Castlemore
Castletownroche
Castleventry
Charleville
Clare Island
Clonakilty
Clondulane
Cloffert
Clonmeen
Cloyne Cathedral
Corkbeg
Creag
Cullen
Desertserges
Donaghmore
Doneraile
Douglas
Drinagh
Drishane
Dromdaleague
Dromtarriff
Dunbullogue
Dunderrow
Dungourney

Dunmanway
Durris
East Ferry
Fanlobbus
Farahy
Fermoy
Frankfield
Garranekinnefeake
Garrycloyne
Glanmire
Glanworth
Glengarriff
Gortroe
Holy Trinity
Inchtermurragh
Inch
Inchigeelagh
Inchinabrackey
Inniscarra
Innishannon
Innishkenny
Kanturk
Kilbolanes
Kilbrin
Kilbrogan
Kilcoe
Kilcredan
Kilcrohane
Kilfaughnabeg
Kilgarriffe
Kilgobbin
Killanully
Killaspugmullane
Killeagh
Killowen
Kilmacabea
Kilmallooda
Kilmeen
Kilmicheal
Kilmocomogue
Kilmoe
Kilmurry
Kilroan
Kilnagross
Kilshannig
Kilworth
Kinneigh
Kinsale
Knocktemple
Leighmoney
Lisgoold
Lislee
Macroom
Marullane
Marshalstown
Middletown

50

Mines
Mitchelstown
Mogeely
Mogeesha
Monanimy
Monkstown
Mourne Abbey
Moviddy
Murragh
Moyross
Nathlash
Nohoval
Queenstown
Rahan
Rathbarry
Rathclaren
Rathcooney
Rathcormack
Rincurran
Ringrone
Rooska
Ross
St. Annes
   (Shandon)
St. Finbarr's
St. Lappan's
St. Luke's
St. Mary's
   (Shandon)
St. Multose
   (Kinsale)
St. Nicholas
St. Paul's
Schull
Shandon
   (St. Anne's)
Shandon
   (St. Mary's)
Skibbereen
Teampol-na-mbocht
Templebodan
Templebready
Templemartin
Templemichael
Templenalarriga
Templenoe
Templomalus
Templequinlan
Templetrine
Timoleague
Tracton
Trullagh
Tullylease
Whitegate
Youghal

Co. Derry
Aghadowey
Aghanloo
Augrim
Badoney
Ballinderry
Ballyeglish
Balygawley
Ballynascreen
Ballynure
Ballyrashane
Ballyscullion
Balteagh
Banagher
Bovevagh
Camusjuxta Bann
Camusjuxta Mourne
Cappagh
Castledawson
Castlerock
Christ Chruch
Claudy
Clooney, All Saints
   (Derry)
Coleraine
Culmore
Cumber Lr.
Cumber Upr.
Derg
Derry Cathedral
Desertmartin
Desertlyn
Dungiven
Eglantine
Errigol
Faughanvale
Fermoyle
Garvagh
Grange
Greenan
Keady
Kilrea
Langfield
Limavady
Maghera
Magherafelt
Mountfield
Muff
Mullhuddert
Portstewart
Rushbrook
St. Augustine's
St. John's
St. Michael's
   (Blackrock)
Tamlaght

Tamlaghard
Tamlaghfinlagan
Templemore
Termoneey
Urney
Woods Chapel

Co. Donegal
Ardara
Ballymore
Bunbeg
Buncranna
Bundoran
Burt
Cashel
Churchtown
Cloncha
Clondehorkey
Clondvaddock
Clonleigh
Clonmany
Convoy
Cornwall
Craigadooish
Cooldaff
Desertegney
Donagh
Donaghmore
   (St. Patrick's)
Donegal
Drumholm
Dunfanaghy
Dunlewey
Fahan
Gartan
Glenalla
Glencolumbkille
Gleneely
Glenties
Gweedore
Inch
Inishkeel
Inver
Kilbarron
Kilcar
Killaghtee
Killea
Killybegs
Kilgarvan
Killymard
Kilmacrenan
Kilteevogue
Laghey
Learbeg
Lech
Letterkenny

Lettermacaward
Lifford
Lough Eske
Meanglass
Mevagh
Milford
Monellan
Mountcharles
Moville
Moy
Newtowncunningham
Pettigoe
Portsalon
Raphoe
Raymoghy
Raymunterdoney
Rossnowlagh
Strangorlar
Taughboyne
Templecrone
Tullaghobegley
Tullyaughnish
Welchtown

Co. Down
Ahaderg
   (Loughbrickland)
Ahavilly
Annalong
Ardglass
Ardkeen
Ardquin
Aughnacloy
Banee
Ballybeen
Ballyculter
Ballyhahalbert
Ballyholme
Ballynahinch
Ballyphillip
Ballywalter
Ballywilliam
Bangor
Bangor Abbey
Bright
Carnalea
Carrowdore
Carryduff
Castlewellian
Clonallen
Comber
Donaghadee
Donaghcloney
Down Cathedral
Down
Dromara

Drumbeg
Drumbo
Drumgath
Drumgooland
Dundonald
Dundrum
Dunsford
Edenderry
Gilford
Green Island
Grey Abbey
Groomsport
Hillsborough
Hollymount
Holywood
Inch
Kilbroney
Kilchief
Kilkeel
Killaney
Killinchy
Killowen
Killyleagh
Kilmood
Kircubbin
Magheradroll
Magherally
Moira
Moneyrea
Newcastle
Newry
Newtownards
Portaferry
Primacy
Rathmullen
Rostrevor
St. Columba's
St. Mary's
  (Newry)
St. Michael's
  (Connor)
St. Molua
St. Patrick's
  (Newry)
Saintfield
Saul
Scarva
Seaford
Seapatrick
Shankill
Strangford
Tullylish
Tullynakill
Tyrella
Warrenpoint

Co. Dublin
Balbriggan
Balrothery
Blackrok
Booterstown
Castleknock
Castlelyons
Chapelizod
Christ Church Cath.
  (Dublin)
Christ Church
  (Dun Laoire)
Christ Church
  (Lesson Park)
Cloghran
Clondalkin
Clonliffe
Clonmethan
Clonsilla
Clontarf
Coolock
Crumlin
Dalkey
Donabate
Donnybrook
  (St. Mary's)
Drumcondra
Dundrum
Finglas
Fre Church
Glasnevin
Glenagarey
Grangegorman
Haroldscross
Holmpatrick
Holy Trinity
  (Killiney)
Howth
Inishtown
Kenure
Killiney
Kill of The Grange
Kilsallaghan
Kilternan
Lucan
Lusk
Magdalene
Malahide
Mariners
  (Dun Laoire)
Milltown
  (St. Phillips)
Monkstown
Mountmerrion
Naul
Newcastle Lyons

Portmarnock
Rahanstown
Rathcoole
Rathfarnham
Rathmichael
Rathmines
St. Aidan's
  (Clonliffe)
St. Andrew's
St. Anne's
St. Audoen's
St. Agustine's
St. Barnabas
St. Bartholomew's
St. Brides
St. Catherine's
St. Columba's
St. Doulough's
St. George's
St. Jame's
St. John's
  (Monkstown)
St. John's
  (Sandymount)
St. Judes
St. Kevin's
St. Luke's
St. Mark's
St. Mary's
St. Mary's
  (Donnybrook)
St. Matthew's
  (Irishtown)
St. Matthia's
St. Michan's
St. Patrick's
  (National Cathedral)
St. Paul's
St. Peter's
St. Philip's
  (Milltown)
St. Stephen's
St. Thomas's
St. Thomas's
  (Foster Avenue)
St. Victor's
St. Werburgs
Santry
Shankill
Stillorgan
Swords
Tallagh
Taney

Trinity
  (Killiney)
Tullow
Whitechurch
Zion Church
  (Rathgar)

Co. Fermanagh
Aghadrumsee
Aghalurcher
Beleek
Benmore
Boho
Castle Archdale
Cleenish
Colaghty
Cooneen
Currin
Derrybrusk
Derryvullen
Devenish
Dromore
Drunkeeran
Enniskillen
Finner
Garvary
Inismacsaint
Inverstown
Killester
Kinawley
Lack
Laragh
Lisbellow
Lisnaskea
Lurgan
Magheracross
Maguiresbridge
Muckross
Mullaghdun
Mullaghfad
Newtown Butler
Ramoan
Rossorry
Sallaghy
Tattykeeran
Tempo
Trillick
Trory

Co. Galway
Ahascragh
Annadown
Aran
Ardrahan
Athenry
Ballinakill

Ballyconree
Ballyhean
Ballymacward
Ballynaboy
Ballynahinch
Ballynakill
Ballyovie
Belcara
   (Drum)
Belclara
Camlough
Castleblackeney
Castlekirke
Cliften
Clonfert
Clontuskert
Eastersnow
Errislannon
Errismore
Eyrecourt
Galway
Gort
Headford
Hollymount
Kilconla
Kilconnell
Kilkerrin
Killannin
Killerroran
Kilmalinoge
Kiltormer
Lickolassy
Monives
Moycullen
Moylough
Moyrus
   (Roundstone)
Moyrus
   (Beauchamp)
Omey
Oranmore
Oughterard
Renvyle
Skerbe
Straid
Tuam
Turlough
Tynagh

Co. Kerry
Aghlish
Ardfert
Ayle
Ballybunion
Ballycushlane
Ballyheigue

Ballylongford
Ballymacelliott
Ballynacourty
Ballysheedy
Brosna
Cahir
Castleisland
Cloghane
Dingle
Dromod
Duagh
Glenbeigh
Kenmare
Kilbolane
Kilcolman
Kilflinn
Kilgarvan
Killarney
Killehenny
Killenlough
Kilentiernan
Killiney
Killorglin
Killurly
Kilmalkedar
Kilmore
Kilmoyley
Kilnaughtin
Listowel
Moore
Muckross
Rattoo
Tarbert
Tralee
Valencia
Ventry
Waterville

Co. Kildare
Athy
Ballinafagh
Ballyburley
Ballycommon
Ballykean
Ballymore Eustace
Ballysax
Ballysonnon
Carbury
Carnalway
Carogh
Castledermot
Celbridge
Clane
Clonsast
Coolcarigan
Donadea

Feighcullen
Fonstown
Garyhinch
Greatconnell
Kilcock
Kilcullen
Kildare
Kilkea
Kill
Killadarry
Killashee
Killeigh
Kilmeage
Lea
Leixslip
Maynooth
Monasterevan
Monasteroris
Mountmellick
Naas
Newbridge
Nurney
Rathangan
Rathmore
Straffon
Thomastown
Timahoe
Timolin

Co. Kilkenny
Burnchurch
Callan
Calry
Castlecomer
Clonmantagh
Clonmore
Clonegam
Cloneyhurke
Colliery
Crosspatrick
Dunmore
Dysart
Ennisnag
Fiddown
Goresbridge
Gowran
Grange
Inistioge
Johnstown
Kells
Kilfane
Kilkenny
Killamery
Kilmacow
Kilmanagh
Knocktopher

Listerlin
Moyne
Odagh
Offerlane
Piltown
Powerstown
St. Canice's
    (Kilkenny)
St. John's
St. Mary's
Shankill
Thomastown
Ullard

Co. Leitrim
Annaduff
Ardcolum
Carrigallen
Clooncumber
Cloone
Corrowallen
Drumlease
Drumlumman
Drumreilly
Drumshambo
Fenagh
Kiltoghert
Kiltubbrid
Kiltyclogher
Manorhamilton
Mohill
Mullagh
Newtowngore
Oughteragh

Co. Laois
Abbeyleix
Ballyfin
Ballyroan
Borris-in-Ossory
Castlefleming
Clonaslee
Coolbanagher
Curraclone
Donaghmore
Durrow
Dysart
Graigue
Killermogh
Killeshin
Lacka
Luggacurren
Maryborough
Mayo
Portarlington
Rathaspick

Rathdowney
Rathsaran
Rosenallis
Stradbally
Timahoe
Timogue

Co. Limerick
Abbeyfeale
Abinton
Adare
Ardcanny
Askeaton
Athlacca
Ballingarry
Ballybrood
Ballylanders
Bruff
Caherconlish
Cahercorney
Cahernanny
Cappagh
Cappamore
Carcomohide
Castlerussell
Corbally
Croagh
Croom
Doon
Drehidtersna
Dromkeen
Effin
Fedamore
Finnoe
Foynes
Galbally
Glin
Kilbehenny
Kilcaskin
Kilcolman
Kilcornan
Kildimo
Kilfergus
Kilfinane
Kilflyn
Kilkeady
Killeedy
Killeely
Kilmallock
Kilmurry
Kilpeacon
Knockaney
Loughill
Mayne
Nantenan
Newcastle West

Oola
Pallasgreen
Particles
Rathkeale
St. John's
    (Limerick)
St. Lawrence's
    (Limerick)
St. Mary's
    (Limerick)
St. Michaels
    (Limerick)
St. Munchins
    (Limerick)
St. Patricks
    (Limerick)
Shangolden
Stradbally
    (South)
Trinity
Tullybrackey

Co. Longford
Abbeylara
Ardagh
Ballycormack
Castlerea
Clongish
Granard
Kilcommock
Kilglass
Killashe
Killoe
Newtownforbes
Rathcline
Shrule
Templemichael

Co. Louth
Ardee
Ballymascanlan
Beaulieu
Collon
Donaghmore
Droheda
St. Mary's
St. Peter's
Dromiskin
Dunany
Dundalk
Dunleer
Finvoy
Haggardstown
Killabban

Killincoole
Kilsaran
Louth
Milltown
St. Mary's
  (Drogheda)
Termonfeckin

Co. Mayo
Achill
Balla
Ballinacourty
Ballinrobe
Ballycroy
Ballysakeery
Barna·
Burrishoole
Cashel
Castlebar
Castleconor
Claremorris
Cong
Crossboyne
Crossmolina
Curroy
Dunfeeney
Emiaghfad
Kilcommon
Kilcommon Erris
Kilcummin
Killala
Kilmaine
Kilmoremoy
Knappagh
Lousiburg
Mallaranny
Neale
Newport
Owenduff
Poulathomas
Slinaun
Swimford
Westford

Co. Meath
Agher
Ardagh
Ardbraccan
Ardnurcher
Athboy
Athlone
  (St. Mary's)
Ballintubber
Ballyadams
Ballyboy
Ballyloughloe

Ballymore
Balrathboyne
Beaupark
Bective
Castlejordan
Castlelost
Castlepollard
Castlerickard
Castletown
Clara
Clonard
Clonfadforan
Clongill
Clonkeen
Clonmore
Collinstown
Clone
Devlin
Donaghpatrick
Drakestown
Down
Drumconrath
Drumcree
Drumraney
Duleek
Dunboyne
Dunshaughlin
Ennisvoffey
Enniskeen
Ferbane
Fertagh
Finnea
Forgney
Foyran
Gallen
Galtrim
Girley
Grange
Jonesborough
Julianstown
Kells
Kentstown
Kilbeggan
Kilbixy
Kilcleagh
Kildalkey
Killallon
Killeagh
Killinagh
Killaucan
Kilmainham Wood
Kilmessan
Kilnagarenagh
Kilshine
Kilskyre
Kiltoom

Kingscourt
Laracor
Lemanaghan
Leney
Loughcrew
Loughran
Mayne
Mellifont
Moybologue
Maydrum
Moyglare
Moyliscar
Moynalty
Mullingar
Navan
Newtownfertullagh
Nobber
Oldcastle
Painstown
Rahan
Raheny
Rathspeck
Rathconnoll
Rathcore
Rathdaire
Rathgraffe
Rathmolyon
Rathowen
Rathoath
Rynagh
Shannonbridge
Skryne
Slane
Stackallen
Stonehall
Synddan
Tara
Tissaran
Trim
Tyrellspass

Co. Monaghan
Aghabog
Ardragh
Ballybay
Carrickmacross
Clones
Clontibret
Crossduff
Drummully
Iniskeen
Killeevan
Kilmore
Maghercross
Monaghan
Mullabrack

57

Newbliss
Rockcorry
Stranoodan
Co. Offaly
Aghancon
Banagher
Birr
Clonbeg
Clonmacnoise
Clonmore
Eglish
Geashill
Killeshill
Killoughy
Lynally
Russagh
Shinrone
Tullamore

Co. Roscommon
Athleague
Aughrim
Boyle
Bumlin
Creagh
Creeve
Croghan
Dunamon
Elphin
Kilbryan
Kilcolman
Kilglass
Killukin
Kilmore
Kilronan
Kiltullagh
Loughglynn
Mount Talbot
Moydow
Oran
Roscommon
Strokestown

Co. Sligo
Achonry
Aghanagh
Ballysodare
Dromard
Drumcliffe
Easkey
Kilglass
Killaraght
Killery
Killoran
Kilmactigue
Knocknaree

Lackan
Lavally
Lisnadill
Riverstown
Rosses
Skreen
Sligo
(St. John's)

Co. Tipperary
Aghnameadle
Ardcroney
Ardfinnan
Ardmayle
Athassell
Ballingarry
Ballintemple
Ballymackey
Ballmurreen
Ballynaclough
Ballysheehan
Borris
Borrisnafarney
Borrisokane
Bourney
Cahir
Cashel
Clogheen
Clonagoose
Clondegad
Clonelty
Clonmel
Clonoulty
Cloughjordan
Cullen
Derrygrath
Donohill
Dundrum
Fennor
Fethard
Golden
Grean
Holycross
Kilcommon
Kilfithmone
Killenaule
Killoscully
Kilmaloge
Kilmastulla
Kilruane
Kilshane
Kilvemnon
Knockgraffon
Lismalin
Lisronagh
Litleton

Lorrha
Loughkeen
Modreeny
Moyne
Neddans
Nenagh
Newchapel
Newport
Rathronan
Rochestown
Roscrea
Shanrahan
Shronnell
Templederry
Templemore
Templeneiry
Templetuohy
Terryglass
Thurles
Tipperary
Toem
Toomavarra
Turbrid
Tulloh
Whitechurch
Youghalarra

Co. Tyrone
Ardstraw
Augher
Ballagh
Barr
Baronscourt
Brackville
Carnteel
Carrickmore
Clanabogan
Clogher
Clogherny
Clonoe
Derrygortreavy
Deryloran
Desertcreat
Donacavey
Donagheady
Donaghendry
Donaghmoine
Drumclamph
Drumakilly
Drumragh
Dungannon
Eglish
Errigal, Kerrogue
Fintona
Fivemiletown
Garvagh

58

Inishmagrath
Kildress
Killyman
Kilskeery
Kiltermon
Learmount
Leckpatrick
Lislimnaghan
Lissan
Omagh
Pomeroy
Sion Mills
Sixmilecross
Stewardstown
Strabane
Tamlaght

Co. Waterford
Ballinakill
Ballybacon
Cappoquin
Castlelane
Castle Ellis
Clashmore
Drumcannon
Dungarvan
Dunhill
Dunmore East
Dysert
Foundains
Guilcagh
Holy Trinity
Kilculliheen
Killea
Kilmeaden
Kiloteran
Kilronan
Kilrossanty
Kilwatermoy
Lismore
Mocollop
Mothel
Portlaw
Ring
St. Olaf
   (Waterford)
St. Patrick's
Stradbally
Tallagh
Templemichael
Tramore
Trinity
Villierstown
Waterford

Co. Wexford
Adamstown
Ardamine
Ballycanew
Ballycarney
Ballyhuskard
Bannow
Branahask
Bunclody
Carn
Clone
Clonmore
Donard
Duncormick
Edermine
Enniscorthy
Ferns
Ferrybank
Fethard
Glascarrig
Glenealy
Gorey
Horetown
Kilbride
Kilcormick
Kildavin
Killane
Killegney
Killena
Killesk
Killinick
Killurin
Kilmuckridge
Kilnahue
Kilnamanagh
Kilpatrick
Kilrush
Kilscoran
Kiltennel
Kinneagh
Kinnegad
Kinnitty
Leskinfere
Monamolin
Monart
Mulrankin
Newcastle
New Ross
Newtownbarry
   (Bunclody)
Old Ross
Rathaspick
Rathmacnee
Rosbercon
Rossdroit
Rosslare

Shillelagh
Tacumshane
Taghmon
Templescobin
Templeshanbo
Templetown
Templeeudigan
Tintern
Tombe
Tomhaggard
Wells
Wexford
Whitechurch

Co. Wicklow
Aghowle
Ardoyne
Arklow
Ashford
Avoca
Ballomaclash
Ballintemple
Ballynure
Baltinglass
Blessington
Bray
   (Christ Church)
Bray
   (St. Paul)
Bray
   (St. James)
Caledon
Carnew
Castlemacadam
Christ Church
   (Bray)
Delgany
Derralossary
Donoughmore
Dunganstown
Dunlavin
Grewstones
Hollywood
Inch
Kilbride, Arklow
Kilbride,
   (Blessington)
Kilbride, Bray
Killiskey
Kilmacoo
Kilpipe
Kiltegan
Lackagh
Laragh
Macreddin
Narraghmore

Newtownmount-
 Kennedy
Powerscourt
Preban
Rathdrum
Redcross
St. James's
 (Bray)
Stratford-on
 Slaney
Tinahely
Wicklow

**Presbyterian
Parishes**

Co. Antrim
Antrim
Armoy
Ballycarny
Ballycastle
Ballyeaston
Ballylinney
Ballymena
Ballymoney
Ballynure
Ballywilliam
Ballymacarrett
 (Belfast)
Ballysillan
Belfast
Fisherwick Place
Rosemary Street
Broadmills
Broughshane
Buckal
Carnmoney
Carrickfergus
Castlereagh
Cliftonville
Cloughwater
Connor
Crumlin
Cullybackey
Dongore
Drumbo
Dundonald
 (Belfast)
Dundron
 (Belfast)
Finvoy
Gilnahurk
 (Belfast)
Glenarn
Glenwheery

Grange
 (Toomebridge)
Kilraught
Larne
Loughmourne
Lylehill
 (Templepatrick)
Masside
Portrush
Raloo
Randalstown
Rasharkin
Templepatrick
Tobberleigh

Co. Armagh
Ahorey
Armagh
Bessbrook
Claldymore
Clare
 (Tandragee)
Cremore
Donacloney
 (Lurgan)
Gilford
Keady
Kingsmills
Knappagh
Lislooney
Loughgall
Lurgan
Markethill
Mountnorris
Newmills
 (Portadown)
Newtown
 hamilton
Portadown
Pountzpass
Richhill
Tandragee
Tullyallen
Vinecash
 (Portadown)

Co. Cavan
Bailieborough
Ballyjamesduff
Bellasis
Cavan
Cootehill
Killeshandra

Co. Cork
Bandon

Cork
Cobh (Queenstown)

Co. Derry
Ballykelly
Banagher
Boveedy
Castledawson
Coleraine
Crossgar
 (Coleraine)
Cumber
 (Claudy)
Derrymore
 (Limavady)
Derry
Draperstown
Drumachose
 (Limavady)
Dunboe
 (Coleraine)
Dungiven
Faughanvale
 (Elinton)
Garvagh
Gortnassy
Killaigh
 (Coleraine)
Kilrea
Lecompher
 (Moneymore)
Limavady
Maghera
Magherafelt
magilligan
Moneymore
Portstewart

Co. Donegal
Ballindrait
Ballyshannon
Buncrana
Burt
Carnone
Carrigart
Convoy
Donegal
Donoughmore
 (Castlefin)
Knowhead
 (Muff)
Letterkenny
Monreagh
Moville
Newtowncunningham
Ramelton

60

Raphoe
St. Johnston
Trentagh
(Kilmacrennan)

Co. Down
Anaghlone
Anahilt
(Hillsborough)
Annalong
Ardaragh (Newry)
Balltdown
(Banbridge)
Ballygilbert
Ballygraney
(Bangor)
Ballynahinch
Ballyroney
(Banbridge)
Ballywalter
Banbridge
Bangor
Carrowdore
(Greyabbey)
Clarkesbridge
(Newry)
Clonduff
(Banbridge)
Clough
(Downpatrick)
Cloughrey
Comber
Conligh
(Newtownards)
Donaghadee
Downpatrick
Dromara
Dromore
Drumbanagher
(Derry)
Drumgooland
Drumlee
(Banbridge)
Edengrove
(Ballynahinch)
Glastry
Groomsport
Hillsborough
Kilkeel
Killinchy
Killyleagh
Kilmore
(Crossgar)
Kirkcubbin
Leitrim
(Banbridge)

Lissera
(Crossgar)
Loughagherry
(Hillsborough)
Loughbrickland
Magherally
(Banbridge)
Millisle
Mourne
(Kilkeel)
Newry
Newtownards
Portaferry
Raffery
(Crossgar)
Rathfriland
Rostrevor
Saintfield
Scarva
Seaforde
Strangeford
Tullylish
(Gilford)
Warrenpoint

Co. Dublin
Abbey Street
Ormond Quay
Clontarf

Co. Fermanagh
Enniskillen
Lisbellow
Pettigo

Co. Galway
Galway

Co. Kerry
Tralee

Co. Laois
Mountmellick

Co. Leitrim
Carrigallen

Co. Limerick
Limerick

Co. Longford
Tully
(Edgeworthstown)

Co. Louth
Corvally
(Dundalk)

Co. Mayo
Dromore
(Ballina)

Co. Monaghan
Ballyalbany
Ballybeg
Ballyhobridge
(Clones)
Broomfield
(Castleblaney)
Cahans
(Ballybay)
Castleblaney
Clones
Clontibret
Corlea
Derryvalley
(Ballybay)
Drumkeen
(Newbliss)
Frankford
(Castleblaney)
Glennan
(Glasslough)
Middletown
(Glasslough)
Monaghan
Newbliss
Scotstown
Stonesbridge
(Newbliss)

Co. Tyrone
Albany
(Stewardstown)
Ardstraw
Aughataire
(Fivemiletown)
Aughnacloy
Ballygawley
Ballygorey
(Cookstown)
Ballynahatty
(Omagh)
Ballyreagh
(Ballygawley)
Brigh
(Stewardstown)
Carland
(Castlecaulfield)
Castlederg
Cleggan
(Cookstown)
Clenanees
(Castlecaulfield)

HOW TO TRACE YOUR IRISH ROOTS

Clogher
Coagh
Cookstown
Donaghheady
 (Strabane)
Drumguin
Dungannon
Edenderry
 (Omagh)
Eglish
 (Dungannon)
Fintona
Gillygooly
 (Omagh)
Gortin

Leckpatrick
 (Strabane)
Minterburn
 (Caledon)
Moy
Newmills
 (Dungannon)
Omagh
Orritor
 (Cookstown)
Pomeroy
Sandholey
 (Cookstown)
Strabane
Urney (Sion Mills)

Co. Waterford
Waterford

Co. Wexford
Wexford

Co. Wicklow
Bray

THE LAMENT OF THE IRISH EMIGRANT
by Lady Dufferin

I'm sitting on the style, Mary, where we sat side by side,
On a bright May morning long ago, when first you were my bride,
The corn was springing fresh and green, and the lark sang loud and high,
And the red was on your lips, Mary, and the love-light in your eye.
The place is little changed, Mary, the day is bright as then,
The lark's long song is in my ear, and the corn is green again,
But I miss the soft clasp of your hand, and your breath warm on my cheek,
And I still keep listening for the words you never more will speak.

* * * * *

'Tis but a step down yonder lane and the little church stands near,
The church where we were wed, Mary, I see the spire from here,
But the graveyard lies between, Mary, and my step might break your rest,
For I've laid you, darling, down to sleep, with your baby on your breast.
I'm very lonely now, Mary, for the poor make no new friends,
But, oh; they love the better still, the few our Father sends,
And you were all I had, Mary, my blessing and my pride,
There's nothing left to care for now, since my poor Mary died.

* * * * *

Yours was the good, brave heart, Mary, that still kept hoping on,
When the trust in God had left my soul, and my arm's young strength had gone,
There was comfort ever on your lips, and the kind look on your brow -,
I bless you, Mary, for the same though you cannot hear me now.
I thank you for the patient smile when your heart was fit to break,
When the hunger pain was gnawing there, and you bid it for my sake,
I bless you for the pleasant word, when your heart was sad and sore -,
Oh; I'm thankful you are gone, Mary, where grief can't reach you more.

* * * * *

I'm bidding you a long farewell, my Mary-kind and true,
But I'll not forget you, darling, in the land I'm going to,
They say there's bread and work for all, and the sun shines always there -.
But I'll not forget old Ireland, were it fifty times as fair.
And often in those grand old woods, I'll sit and shut my eyes,
And my heart will travel back again, to the place where Mary lies,
And I think I'll see the little stile where we sat side by side,
And the springing corn, and the bright May morn when first you were my bride.

These words would reflect the thoughts of many an Irish emigrant, during those black Famine days.

Here are some useful addresses to help you with your research:

Genaelogical Office,
2 Kildare Street,
Dublin 2.
Tel: (01) 765521

General Register Office,
Joyce House,
8-11 Lombard Street,
Dublin 2
Tel: (01) 711000
(Births, Marriages and Deaths, from January 1st 1864)

Irish Valuation Office,
6 Ely Place,
Dublin 2.
Tel: (01) 763211
(useful to trace present day owner of land)

National Library of Ireland,
Kildare Street,
Dublin 2.
Tel: (01) 765521
(a must for the researcher)

Ordanance Survey Office,
Phoenix Park,
Dublin
Tel: (01) 213171
(maps)

Public Records Office,
The Four Courts,
Dublin 7
Tel: (01) 733833
(The Tithe Applotment Books, which contain the 1820s Census Records)

Public Records Office of Northern Ireland,
66 Balmoral Avenue,
Belfast BT9 6 YN.
Tel: (084) 661621
(The Tithe Applotment Books for: Antrim. Armagh. Down, Derry, Tyrone and Fermanagh)

State Paper Office,
Dublin Castle,
Dublin 2.
Tel: (01) 792777
(convict records and details of those sentenced to transportation; 1798 rebellion reports and other very interesting documents)

Records of the different Churches

Roman Catholic Church.
Records are in the custody of the Parish Priest of Parish concerned.
Church of Ireland or Protestant Church.
Some records are in the custody of The Rector, at local level.
Other records at: Representative Church Body Library,
Braemor Park,
Rathgar,
Dublin.

Presbyterian Church.
Some records at local level,
also contact: Presbyterian Historical Society,
               Church House,
               Fisherwick Place,
               Belfast BT1 6DW.

Quaker Records.
Society of Friends' Library,
6 Eustace Street,
Dublin.

There are many good record books on, Huguenot and Paletine families in The National Library.
The above addresses should be of assistance to your search. If in doubt, the staff of the libraries and other State offices will be very happy to advise you.

MY WISH FOR YOU

I hope in these pages I have given you some useful hints, in your ancestral search and as I have already stated do as much homework as possible, before making your journey "Home" as you will have so much more time to enjoy the fruits of your research. Even if you do not find any relatives I think you will find Irish people very friendly and that Ireland is a very beautiful country. It often occurs to me that if our ancestors could see how far we have come, they are no longer the oppressed and downtrodden people they were in the unhappy past.

All I can do now is wish you "Good Luck" in your search of your Irish roots, and hope you will enjoy an unforgettable Irish vacation.

AN OLD IRISH BLESSING

May the road rise to meet you.
  May the wind be always at your back,
May God hold you in the palm of His hand.

Rock of Cashel Co Tipperary — (Courtesy of Bord Fáilte)

Jaunting Car, Killarney, Co Kerry. —— (Courtesy of Bord Fáilte)